THE

DRAGON
ATLAS

For Io—A. C.

For all my cutest nephews
and nieces—P. Q. P.

LAURENCE KING
First published in the United States in 2024 by Laurence King

ISBN: 978-1-510-23060-6

10 9 8 7 6 5 4 3 2 1

Printed in China

Laurence King
An imprint of
Hachette Children's Group
Part of Hodder and Stoughton
Carmelite House
50 Victoria Embankment
London EC4Y 0DZ

An Hachette UK Company
www.hachette.co.uk
www.hachettechildrens.co.uk
www.laurenceking.com

*The stories and information in this book come from ancient traditional
tales and folklore of many peoples around the world. In each case,
the author has chosen one retelling, although there may be
different versions of each story or tradition.*

THE DRAGON ATLAS

LEGENDARY DRAGONS OF THE WORLD

WORDS BY
ANNA CLAYBOURNE

ILLUSTRATIONS BY
PHAM QUANG PHUC

Laurence King

CONTENTS

THE WORLD OF DRAGONS

On an old copper globe, made around the year 1510, is a famous inscription: HIC SVNT DRACONES. It's Latin for "Here be dragons." This is written near the coast of Southeast Asia, warning of the dangerous monsters that explorers and sailors might find there.

However, this warning might as well have been written all over the globe. The fact is, wherever you travel, from the icy Arctic to tropical jungles, from east to west and north to south, you'll find tales, rumors, and warnings of dragons. Since ancient times, even peoples who lived oceans apart, and never knew of each other's existence, have described scaly, fiery, flying, or crawling beasts, with deadly appetites, mysterious abilities, or magical powers.

It seems that dragons have always shared our world. They may often be out of sight, hiding in mountain caves or craters, lurking in deep water, or flying over us by night. But they are found in the stories, myths, and legends of almost every culture on Earth, and many people believe they really exist, too. Do you?

ANF VROIN
HIC SVNT
DRACONES

WHAT IS A DRAGON?

There are many types of dragons, but they all have several things in common. They usually resemble giant snakes, lizards, or crocodiles, with long, scaly bodies and tails. Some have wings and fly, some don't, and not all dragons breathe fire—but almost all have a recognizable dragon's head, with large nostrils, gleaming eyes, and horns or a crest. Dragons are usually large creatures, but there are some tiny enough to sit in your hand.

TAKE CARE!

Dragons, like people, can be good or bad. Many, especially those found in Asia, are kind, helpful creatures who look after humans and keep watch over the natural world. But there are also many dangerous, deadly, and downright evil dragons, who think nothing of snapping up passers-by or scorching the land with their burning breath. Even good-natured dragons can turn nasty if you annoy them. So, always be on your guard, take care not to disturb them . . . and prepare yourself with the useful dragon guide on page 48 before you go dragon-spotting.

EUROPE

Welcome to Europe, the second smallest continent in the world, bordered by many bodies of water. Across this continent, from the frozen north to the balmy Mediterranean, you'll find countless dragons in local folklore, myths, and fairy tales. They're also reflected in place names, such as Dragon Hill in England, Dragon's Cave in Croatia, and Greece's Dragon Lakes.

Many of these dragons belong to a particular type, known to dragon experts as the European dragon. They tend to resemble a giant snake or lizard, usually with four legs, horns, and a long tail. Often, these dragons fly on leathery, bat-like wings, but some have no wings and slither along the ground. They may breathe fire or exhale deadly poison. Many dwell in caves, but some prefer forests, lakes, or the sea.

Wherever you may find them, take care: European dragons can be extremely dangerous, especially if guarding treasure. You have been warned!

ICELAND

The **STOOR WORM'S** teeth and burning body became the lands of Orkney, Shetland, Faroe, and Iceland.

FAROE ISLANDS

SHETLAND ISLANDS

SCOTLAND

ORKNEY ISLANDS

The Islands of Orkney, where Assipattle battled the mighty **STOOR WORM.**

ENGLAND

WALES

DRAGON HILL

Home of **Y DDRAIG GOCH**, the brave red dragon of Wales.

BASQUE COUNTRY

Beware the fearsome seven-headed **HERENSUGE** from the Basque country.

SPAIN

FAFNIR, a Norse dragon, hoards its treasure here.

SWEDEN

FINLAND

RUSSIA

NORWAY

Here dwells the **ZMEY GORYNYCH**, an evil shape-shifting dragon.

DENMARK

POLAND

Kraków was home to the **WAWEL DRAGON** until he exploded!

GERMANY

The **DRAGON LAKES** are said to have been made by dragons throwing rocks at each other.

UKRAINE

Watch out for the unusual river-dwelling **TARASQUE.**

CROATIA

FRANCE

ITALY

DRAGON CAVE on the island of Brac.

GREECE

ASSIPATTLE AND THE STOOR WORM

THE DEFEAT OF A GIANT DRAGON

ORKNEY, SCOTLAND

In the legends of the Orkney Islands, the Stoor Worm was an enormous sea dragon who terrorized the world. It could swallow and crush ships in an instant and crawl onto the land, sweeping whole towns into the sea. Wherever the Stoor Worm rested its mountain-sized head on the shore, it commanded the local people to bring it seven young women to eat every Saturday.

One day, the Stoor Worm arrived at a beautiful kingdom and made its usual demands. The people living there had to sacrifice their daughters to the dragon or risk their city being destroyed.

But when the king's own daughter was due to be eaten, he decided enough was enough. He announced that the person who killed the Stoor Worm would be awarded his magic sword, Sickersnapper, along with his kingdom.

A young farmer's son named Assipattle declared that he would take on the challenge. Everyone laughed, but Assipattle took some hot peat from the fire and rode his father's fastest horse to where the dragon lay. Using the king's boat, he sailed toward the monster, who opened up its vast mouth and swallowed the boat whole with Assipattle in it.

Deep inside the Stoor Worm's stomach, the boy threw out the burning peat, setting fire to the dragon's insides. It roared in pain, breathing flames and thick smoke that filled the sky, hurling Assipattle and his boat back out of its mouth and onto the beach.

The king, his people, and Assipattle clambered up a hill to watch as the dragon burned up, writhing and spluttering in agony.

Its huge, forked tongue shot out of its mouth, carving a deep trench that became the Baltic Sea. Its teeth fell out, forming the Orkney, Shetland, and Faroe Islands. And finally, its burned body, alight with flames, curled up and became the land of Iceland. As the king had promised, he gave Assipattle his sword and his kingdom. Assipattle married the king's daughter, and the people rejoiced that the Stoor Worm was no more.

HERENSUGE
BASQUE COUNTRY

In ancient Basque folktales, the Herensuge is a monstrous dragon with seven heads. Each head is a baby dragon, which grows to full size, then drops off to become another Herensuge. There are many tales about this fearsome fire-spitting beast. In one, a mother gives her son a cake to take on his travels. When he kindly offers it to a poor old woman, she gives him a magic stick that can kill any monster. He comes to a town that is being terrorized by a Herensuge and uses the stick to kill the dragon, hitting it once on each head.

WAWEL DRAGON
POLAND

In a famous Polish legend, the Wawel Dragon lived in a cave under Wawel Hill, site of the royal castle in the city of Kraków. The people of the city lived in fear, and to stop the dragon from eating humans, they had to feed it sheep and cows every day. King Krakus offered his crown to anyone who could destroy the dragon. Many tried and failed, until a young shoemaker named Skuba stuffed a sheep with sulfur and fed it to the dragon. The sulfur burned the beast's throat, and it ran to the river and drank so much water that it exploded! To this day, you can visit the cave below Wawel Hill and see a statue of the dragon that breathes real fire.

ZMEY GORYNYCH
RUSSIA AND UKRAINE

The Zmey Gorynych, or "dragon of the mountains," appears in many old Russian and Ukrainian stories and songs. A huge dragon with three horned heads, seven tails, and glittering copper claws, it was known for setting fire to villages and transforming itself into a handsome human to trick and kidnap young women. The famous *bogatyr* (hero) Dobrynya Nikitich fought the Zmey, but the dragon begged for mercy, promising it would never attack anyone again. Dobrynya released it, but the evil Zmey soon went back to its old ways. So, Dobrynya went back a second time and finally slew the Zmey after an epic three-day battle.

FAFNIR
SCANDINAVIA

Fafnir, the mighty dragon of Norse mythology, was not always a dragon. He was once a *dvergr*, a magical elf-like creature, and the son of King Hreidmar. Fafnir's brother, Otr, could change into an otter, and while in this form, the god Loki killed him, thinking he was a real otter. To make amends, Loki had to give Hreidmar a hoard of gold. But the gold was cursed to destroy whoever owned it. Desperate to grab it for himself, Fafnir killed his father, escaped to a cave in the wilderness and became a terrifying wingless dragon, breathing out poison to keep everyone away from his precious treasure.

TARASQUE
FRANCE

Long ago in the south of France, the fearsome Tarasque roamed the banks of the Rhône river. This strange six-legged dragon resembled a cross between a fish and a turtle, with spikes on its back, sharp teeth, and a swishing, stinging tail. It often entered the river, where it would overturn boats and devour people as they fell out. Many brave knights tried to kill the Tarasque, but none succeeded. Finally, the people asked Saint Martha to help. She managed to tame the beast with her kindness and led it away from the river. The nearby town of Tarascon is named after the famous local dragon.

THE RED DRAGON
WALES

The red dragon (*Y Ddraig Goch* in Welsh) has been the symbol of Wales for over a thousand years. An old legend tells how King Lludd was bothered by a local red dragon having a noisy fight with a white dragon. To keep them quiet, he captured them and buried them under the hill Dinas Emrys. Much later, King Vortigern built a castle on the hill, but it kept falling down. A young boy told him that this was because of the dragons underneath, so Vortigern dug down to find them. The dragons awoke and began fighting again. At last, the brave red dragon defeated its enemy and became the symbol of Vortigern's kingdom.

MEET THE DRAGONS

Everyone thinks that they know what a dragon looks like, yet these fabulous beasts come in an amazingly wide range of shapes and sizes, with many different features and magical abilities. Each continent and corner of the globe has its own typical style of dragon, with many different variations. These two pages are your guide to the main types of dragons found around the world, including those you'll encounter in this book.

EUROPEAN OR WESTERN DRAGONS

This species of dragon, found in European folktales and legends since ancient times, is a large, scaly beast, usually with four legs and two wings. It has a large head with sharp teeth, large nostrils, and several horns or spikes. These dragons can usually fly and often breathe fire.

Variations on the European dragon include:

Wyvern: A small two-legged dragon. It often has a long, snakelike tail, which may be tipped with a venomous sting.

Cockatrices and **Basilisks:** Similar to a Wyvern but with the head of a rooster. Though small, they can kill with their deadly breath or touch, or even just with a glance.

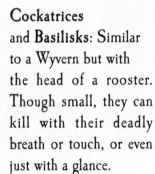

Dragonet: A small or young dragon. They can be tiny but can still kill their enemies with their poisonous breath or acidic, burning blood.

Orms, Wyrms, and **Lindworms:** Long snake-shaped dragons. Some have a crest, mane, or row of spikes along their backs.

ASIAN OR EASTERN DRAGONS

Dragons are a central part of many Asian myths, legends, and folktales. In China, Japan, Korea, Vietnam and nearby lands, the typical dragon resembles a huge, scaly snake with four legs and a dragon's head.

The Cambodian **Neak** often has no legs.

AFRICAN DRAGONS

Found in Egyptian mythology, Ethiopian legends, and local folktales all over Africa, many African dragons look like giant reptiles, with dinosaur or lizard-like features, sometimes combined with parts of other animals. For example, the **Grootslang** of South Africa is a monstrous deadly beast that is part snake and part elephant.

HORNED SERPENTS

All over the Americas, traditional tales and ancient myths feature horned serpents, and they are sometimes found in other places, too, such as Africa. These giant snakelike creatures can also have feathers or feathered wings. Some have eyes that glow with fire, while others fly through the air, leaving a fiery trail.

The Aztec god **Quetzalcoatl** often appears as a horned serpent.

The **Arwe**, an ancient dragon of Ethiopia, was a giant serpent with a horned dragon head.

HOW MANY HEADS?

Like other animals, most dragons have only one head—but some have more. The **Zmey Gorynych** has three, and the **Kuzuryu** of Japan has nine. But they are all beaten by the ancient Greek **Hesperian Dragon**, who guarded the goddess Hera's orchard and had a hundred heads.

Beware the fearsome
NINKI NANKA
that lurks in West
Africa's swamps.

SENEGAL

THE GAMBIA

Take care not to get
snapped up by the
dinosaur-like
GBAHALI.

LIBERIA

MOKELE-MBEMBE
roams the waters of the
mighty Congo River.

CONGO RIVER

*DEMOCRATIC
REPUBLIC
OF THE
CONGO*

AFRICA

*A*frica is a vast continent filled with dense jungles,
enormous deserts, remote mountain ranges, and mighty
roaring rivers, where many a fierce dragon has freedom to roam.

Long ago, explorers described Ethiopia, in eastern Africa, as
the land where dragons came from. But dragons are reported in
many other parts of Africa, too, from the great Congo River to
the vast swamps of West Africa, and towering Drakensberg, or
Dragon Mountain, in Lesotho.

Some African dragons resemble ancient dinosaurs, and some say
that dinosaur-like beasts could still be living here. Others share
features with African creatures such as crocodiles, elephants, or
even giraffes. But whatever they look like, beware: Many of these
dragons are to be feared. If they don't swallow you in an instant,
the mere sight of one could foretell disaster.

Drakensberg, or Drago[n]
Mountain, where
Princess Thakane slew
the **NANABOLELE**

The **KHODUMODUMO,**
an enormous-mouthed
dragon-like beast.

LESOTHO

SOUTH AFRICA

Howick Falls, South
Africa, home of the
INKANYAMBA
horse-dragon.

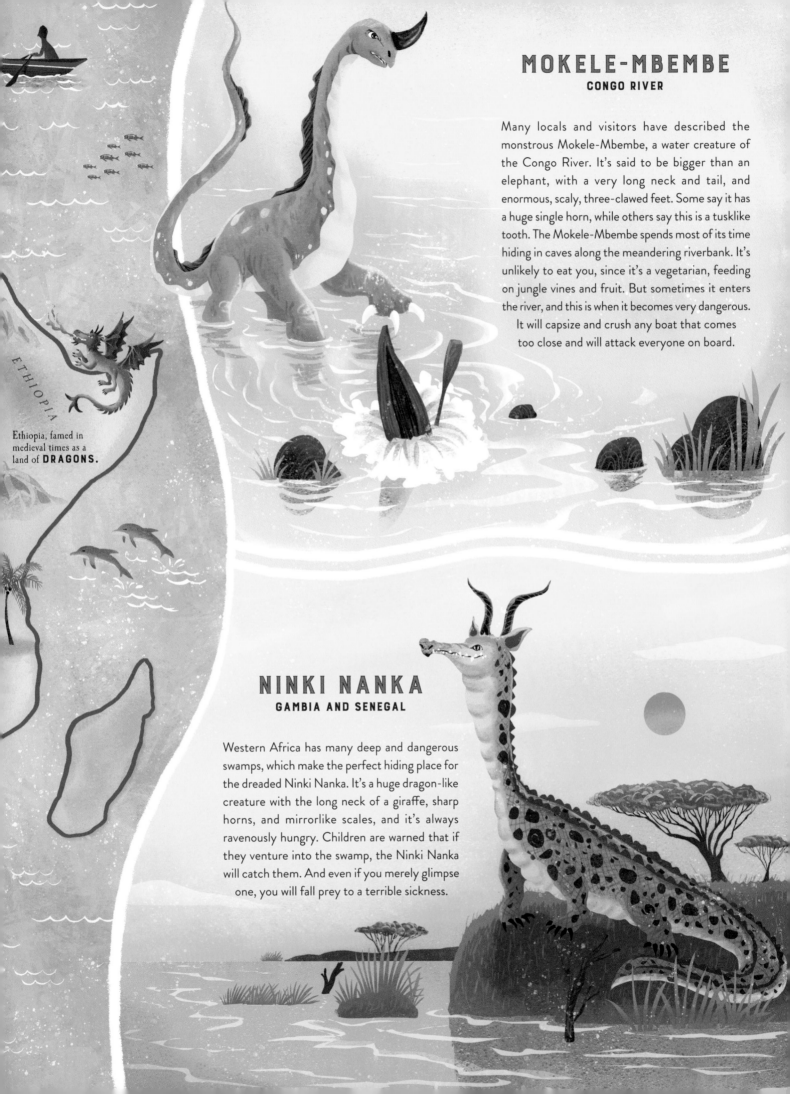

MOKELE-MBEMBE
CONGO RIVER

Many locals and visitors have described the monstrous Mokele-Mbembe, a water creature of the Congo River. It's said to be bigger than an elephant, with a very long neck and tail, and enormous, scaly, three-clawed feet. Some say it has a huge single horn, while others say this is a tusklike tooth. The Mokele-Mbembe spends most of its time hiding in caves along the meandering riverbank. It's unlikely to eat you, since it's a vegetarian, feeding on jungle vines and fruit. But sometimes it enters the river, and this is when it becomes very dangerous. It will capsize and crush any boat that comes too close and will attack everyone on board.

ETHIOPIA

Ethiopia, famed in medieval times as a land of **DRAGONS.**

NINKI NANKA
GAMBIA AND SENEGAL

Western Africa has many deep and dangerous swamps, which make the perfect hiding place for the dreaded Ninki Nanka. It's a huge dragon-like creature with the long neck of a giraffe, sharp horns, and mirrorlike scales, and it's always ravenously hungry. Children are warned that if they venture into the swamp, the Ninki Nanka will catch them. And even if you merely glimpse one, you will fall prey to a terrible sickness.

INKANYAMBA
SOUTH AFRICA

The Inkanyamba is a giant water serpent with a horse or dragon-like head, said to live in waterfalls and lakes in the KwaZulu-Natal area of South Africa. It can rear up on its tail to a towering height and fly using its bat-like or flipper-shaped wings. According to local wisdom, it is most active in the summer, when it soars through the sky from one waterfall or lake to another in search of a mate. If it can't find one, it becomes angry, and its fury causes powerful summer rainstorms or tornadoes.

KHODUMODUMO
LESOTHO

In the traditional tales of the Basotho people of Lesotho, the Khodumodumo is a mysterious, hungry reptilian monster. Its massive mouth contains many sharp tongues, which it uses to stab its prey. According to an old legend, it once went on a rampage and devoured all the humans and their animals. Just one woman escaped, by hiding in a dunghill, where the Khodumodumo could not smell her. She gave birth to a son, who grew to adulthood in a single day and went to find the monster. Dodging its deadly tongues, he cut it open and set everyone free again.

GBAHALI
LIBERIA

In the dense jungles of Liberia, locals often report sightings of the terrifying Gbahali. This dragon-like river creature resembles a giant spiky-backed crocodile or lizard up to 33 feet (10 metres) long, but instead of crawling, it walks upright on long legs. It's said to emerge from rivers to grab people or animals, then drag them under the water. Some people believe it's an unknown species yet to be discovered and could be a long-lost relative of the Postosuchus, a fierce prehistoric reptile that lived at the same time as the dinosaurs.

THAKANE THE DRAGON-SLAYER

THE PRINCESS WHO SLEW A DRAGON FOR ITS SKIN

LESOTHO

In an old legend from Lesotho, Thakane was the daughter of a great Basotho chief. Sadly, her parents died, leaving her to care for her two little brothers. According to tradition, boys wore skins from animals their fathers had hunted. With no father to do this, Thakane went hunting and gave her brothers lion and buffalo skins to wear. But the spoiled princes complained that as the sons of a chief, they should wear Nanabolele skins.

This was no easy task, for a Nanabolele is a fierce, glowing underwater dragon. Nonetheless, Thakane took her spear and set off along the river to find one. After many days, she came to a wide pool, where an old woman came out of the water. She led Thakane below the surface to a hidden underwater village where the Nanabolele lived and hid her in a hole. When the creatures returned, they roared, "We smell a human! Where is it?" But they couldn't find anyone and fell asleep.

Thakane sneaked out of the hole and quickly killed a dragon, skinned it, and packed up the skin to take home. Before she left, the old woman gave her a magic pebble. "The other Nanabolele will chase you," she said. "But throw down this pebble, and it will become a mountain that they cannot climb." Thakane took the pebble and used it to stop the dragons whenever they caught up with her. At last, she made it back to her village, and her brothers got their dragon-skin outfits.

THE DRAGON'S LAIR

Where do dragons live? Dragons tend to be big, and they are usually solitary and dwell alone. Because of this, they're often found in wild, remote places with plenty of space: mountains, hills and caves, forests, lakes or swamps. But just as there are many kinds of dragons, there's a wide variety of lairs, dens, and other places where they like to make their homes.

A CAVE FULL OF TREASURE

Many dragons guard hoards of treasure. A remote cave is the perfect lair since it keeps their loot out of sight. The famous Norse dragon Fafnir, for example, fled to a remote cave to protect his stolen treasure. Africa's fearsome Grootslang is said to live in a deep, dark cave in Richtersveld, filled with diamonds and precious stones. And the gold-guarding dragon in the Old English tale of *Beowulf* lived in an old underground burial chamber.

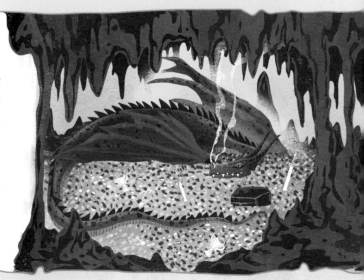

CASTLE DRAGONS

Old castles are often linked to famous dragons. Poland's famous Wawel dragon was said to live beneath Kraków Castle. In another legend a large dragon took over Denbigh Castle in Wales, and made its home in the great hall.

WATER DRAGONS

In many parts of the world, especially Asia and Oceania, dragons are usually associated with water. They live in rivers, ponds, or lakes or in the seas and oceans. The Tarasque of France was often found submerged in the Rhône river, while Ryujin, a Japanese sea-god dragon, lived in an undersea coral palace.

HIGH IN THE SKY

Meanwhile, some dragons spend all their time in the sky, searching for food or roaming from place to place. In parts of Asia, sky-dwelling dragons control the winds, clouds, and rain. The Tianlong, or Heavenly Dragon, of Chinese folklore guards the gates of heaven and lives in a sky mansion made of clouds.

In Greek mythology, the goddess Athena fought the dragon Draco and threw him into the sky, where he remains as the constellation Draco.

UNUSUAL LAIRS

Of course, some dragons do things differently and have their own unique homes.

The Zilant is a Wyvern-like dragon from Tatarstan in Russia. To guard the city of Kazan he made himself a nest of iron chains, suspended from 12 oak trees.

After being caught in a river as a tiny baby, a famous English dragon named the Lambton Worm grew to a huge size and coiled itself around a hill.

Tiny Pyrausta are insect-sized fire animals from Cyprus. They are described in an ancient Roman book as four-legged winged beasts and are often thought to be miniature dragons. They live in flames inside metalworking furnaces and die if they fly too far from the heat.

ASIA

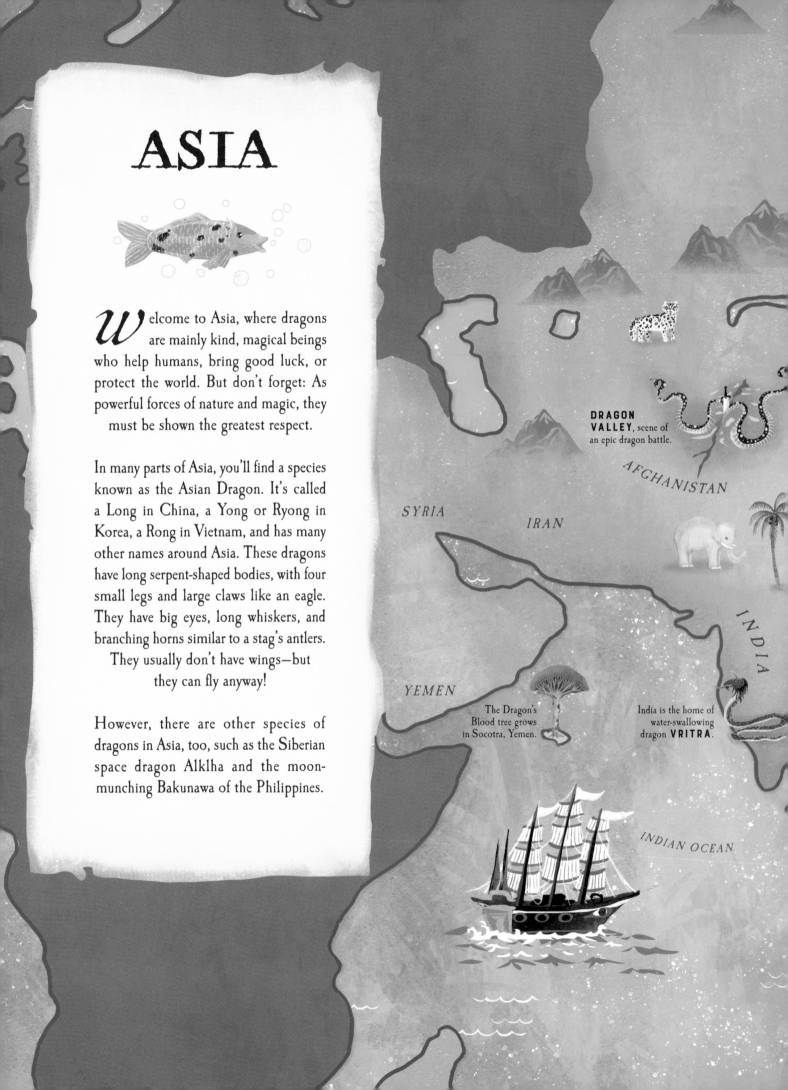

Welcome to Asia, where dragons are mainly kind, magical beings who help humans, bring good luck, or protect the world. But don't forget: As powerful forces of nature and magic, they must be shown the greatest respect.

In many parts of Asia, you'll find a species known as the Asian Dragon. It's called a Long in China, a Yong or Ryong in Korea, a Rong in Vietnam, and has many other names around Asia. These dragons have long serpent-shaped bodies, with four small legs and large claws like an eagle. They have big eyes, long whiskers, and branching horns similar to a stag's antlers. They usually don't have wings—but they can fly anyway!

However, there are other species of dragons in Asia, too, such as the Siberian space dragon Alklha and the moon-munching Bakunawa of the Philippines.

DRAGON VALLEY, scene of an epic dragon battle.

AFGHANISTAN

SYRIA

IRAN

INDIA

YEMEN

The Dragon's Blood tree grows in Socotra, Yemen.

India is the home of water-swallowing dragon **VRITRA**.

INDIAN OCEAN

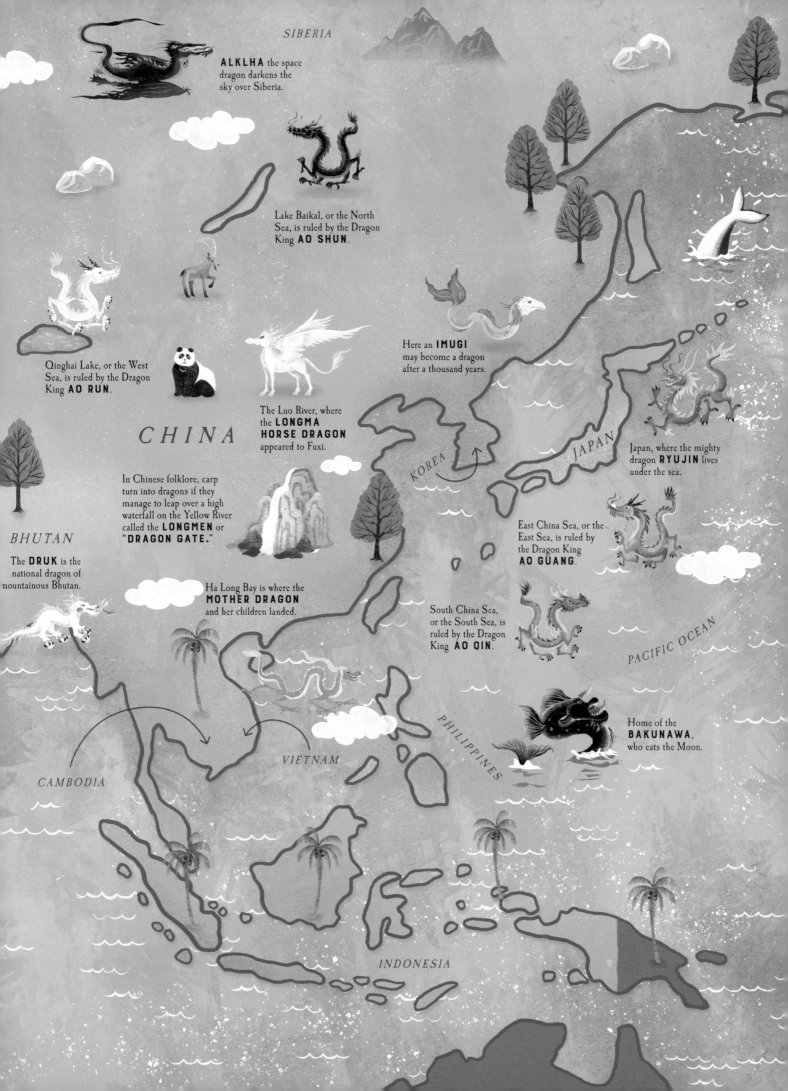

SIBERIA

ALKLHA the space dragon darkens the sky over Siberia.

Lake Baikal, or the North Sea, is ruled by the Dragon King **AO SHUN**.

Qinghai Lake, or the West Sea, is ruled by the Dragon King **AO RUN**.

CHINA

The Luo River, where the **LONGMA HORSE DRAGON** appeared to Fuxi.

Here an **IMUGI** may become a dragon after a thousand years.

KOREA

JAPAN

Japan, where the mighty dragon **RYUJIN** lives under the sea.

In Chinese folklore, carp turn into dragons if they manage to leap over a high waterfall on the Yellow River called the **LONGMEN** or "**DRAGON GATE.**"

East China Sea, or the East Sea, is ruled by the Dragon King **AO GUANG**.

BHUTAN

The **DRUK** is the national dragon of mountainous Bhutan.

Ha Long Bay is where the **MOTHER DRAGON** and her children landed.

South China Sea, or the South Sea, is ruled by the Dragon King **AO QIN**.

PACIFIC OCEAN

PHILIPPINES

Home of the **BAKUNAWA**, who eats the Moon.

CAMBODIA

VIETNAM

INDONESIA

THE CHINESE LONG
CHINA

Dragons are very important in Chinese culture and legends. The dragon, or Long, is one of the 12 signs of the Chinese zodiac and a symbol of good luck, strength, kindness, and success. Dragons often appear in decorations, art, and traditional dances performed by a long line of dancers in a dragon costume. These highly skilled performances now take place in many Asian countries, including Singapore.

THE FOUR DRAGON KINGS
CHINA

The Longwang, or Dragon Kings, are the rulers of the four "seas" around ancient China (which include two large lakes). These dragons can change shape to take the form of a human or sometimes a towering waterspout. They live in glass palaces under the seas, eating pearls and precious stones, with sea creatures as their guards and servants. Each dragon represents a different point of the compass and season of the year. The four Dragon Kings are:

NORTH
AO SHUN, THE BLACK DRAGON
Lake Baikal
Winter

EAST
AO GUANG, THE AZURE DRAGON
East China Sea
Spring

WEST
AO RUN, THE WHITE DRAGON
Qinghai Lake
Fall

SOUTH
AO QIN, THE RED DRAGON
South China Sea
Summer

FUXI AND THE LONGMA

HOW A DRAGON SHARED ITS WISDOM

LUO RIVER, CHINA

In Chinese mythology, the ancient god Fuxi was human-shaped, with a long dragon tail. He was the father of all humans and lived on Earth to care for them. He taught them how to fish, farm, and cook; how to play music, write, and how to make silk. But even the great Fuxi did not know everything.

One day, as Fuxi was fishing in the Luo River, the water began to swirl and bubble, and a strange creature rose up out of it. It had the head of a dragon, the body of a horse, and a pair of beautiful wings. It was a Longma, or Dragon Horse. The Longma stood on the surface of the water, then walked toward Fuxi, bowing its head in respect. As it came closer, Fuxi saw eight symbols on its back. He stored the symbols in his memory, as the Longma lifted up its two front feet and flew into the sky.

Fuxi quickly found a stick and drew the symbols in the muddy riverbank. He studied the symbols for many days, until he finally made sense of them. He used them to create the *I Ching*, a book that showed how to understand the ways of the world, read the stars and planets, and foretell the future. Ever since then, seeing a Longma has been the sign of a great, wise leader.

DRUK
BHUTAN

The Druk, or Thunder Dragon, is the national symbol of Bhutan, a small country between China and India. In Dzongkha, the country's language, Bhutan is called Druk Yul, or "Thunder Dragon Land." Its people are the Drukpa, or the Thunder Dragon People, and the Druk appears on the country's flag. This kind, wise dragon is usually white, a symbol of purity, and is said to guide people toward truth and goodness. Its fiery roar creates the sound of thunder, which is often heard in mountainous Bhutan's many lighting storms.

IMUGI
KOREA

Like other Asian lands, Korea has many dragons, known as Yong or Ryong. But it also has Imugi, who are not true dragons, but might one day become them. They are serpent-shaped sea creatures similar to dragons, but with no horns and (some say) no legs. To become a true dragon, an Imugi must live for a thousand years, then wait for a yeouiju, a magical, round jewel, to fall from Heaven. If it catches a yeouiju, the Imugi will finally become a dragon and gain the ability to fly. Imugi are kind, shy creatures, and if you see one, it will bring you fabulously good luck.

BAKUNAWA
PHILIPPINES

In the Philippines, the mighty Bakunawa is believed to cause earthquakes and eclipses of the Moon. This enormous beast is said to have wings, sharklike gills, and a vast mouth and to live in the deepest, darkest parts of the ocean. In the beginning, the legends say, the world had seven moons. But every so often, the Bakunawa would rise up out of the sea and devour one of them. At last, there was only one moon left. When the Bakunawa appeared again and tried to eat it, the people decided to take action. They all ran toward the sea, banging pots and pans and shouting. They scared the Bakunawa away. To this day, you can still see its toothmarks on our last remaining moon.

HA LONG BAY AND THE MOTHER DRAGON

THE STORY OF THE DRAGONS WHO SAVED VIETNAM

VIETNAM

Ha Long Bay is one of the most beautiful places in Vietnam: A sheltered bay filled with hundreds of dramatic limestone islands and tiny islets jutting high out of the azure sea. Its name, Ha Long, means "descending dragon," thanks to the dragons who saved the Vietnamese people, according to ancient legend.

Long, long ago, when Vietnam was a newly formed country, its people were being attacked by merciless invaders, who came across the ocean. Seeing their struggle, the gods sent the Mother Dragon and her children to help them. As the attackers approached the coast, the dragons swooped down out of the sky, breathing jets of fire. Emeralds and precious jade rocks fell from the dragons' mouths into the sea, and where they landed, islands sprang up, blocking the ships' route to the shore. Scorched by fire and smashed against the rocks, the invaders retreated, never to return, and Vietnam was left in peace.

Then the Mother Dragon looked around and saw how beautiful the bay was and how hardworking and honest the people were. So, instead of returning to the sky, she decided to stay. She and her children transformed into humans and came to live with the Vietnamese people, teaching them to work their land, grow crops, and keep cattle. And to this day, the bay of many islands is known as Ha Long Bay, the place where the dragons came down to live on Earth.

THE LEGEND OF DRAGON VALLEY

HERE LIES A DEADLY DRAGON TURNED TO STONE

AFGHANISTAN

In a deep mountain valley in Afghanistan lies a huge serpent-shaped rock, split in two along its length. According to local legends, a monstrous dragon once lived here. It demanded a daily diet of humans and camels, and the people were powerless to get rid of it. Many brave heroes came to fight it, but none could even get close. As soon as they approached, it burned them to ashes with its fiery breath.

None, that is, until the great Arabian warrior Ali ibn Abi Talib came to the rescue with his sword Zulfiqar, the "spine-splitter." As Ali came near, the dragon blew out a jet of fire,

and everyone thought Ali would be roasted alive. But then something magical happened. So good and noble was Ali, the flames could not harm him. As they touched him, they turned into tulip petals and fluttered to the ground. Ali lifted the mighty Zulfiqar and sliced the beast in two.

With a thunderous groan, the dragon sank to the ground and became a ridge of stone with a deep crack along the middle—and there it lies to this day. A stream that runs through the fissure is said to be made of the dragon's tears of remorse. This valley is known as Darya-e Adjahar, or Dragon Valley.

28

VRITRA
INDIA

In the Hindu mythology of India, Vritra is an enormous, evil dragon, one of the Asuras, the enemies of the gods. Long and snake-shaped, Vritra is so big that he can encircle mountains. Long ago, he caused disaster for humans by sucking in all the water from the Earth: All the rivers, lakes, and streams and even the rain from the air, until drought ravaged the land, the plants withered, and the humans and animals were dying of thirst. Indra, king of the gods, set out to fight Vritra using a lightning bolt as a weapon. They battled for many days, but at last Indra pierced Vritra's side. The dragon's body burst open, and all the water came flooding out, bringing life back to the world.

ALKLHA
SIBERIA, RUSSIA

Many dragons are big. Some are truly vast. But there is probably no other dragon as terrifyingly gigantic as Alklha. In the legends of the Buryat people of Siberia, in the Asian part of Russia, Alklha is a space dragon, who lives among the stars. Its black wings spread so wide that they can cover the sky and block out all the light, and it causes solar eclipses by swallowing the Sun. Luckily for humans, the Sun always reappears, because it's so hot that Alklha is soon forced to spit it out.

THE DRAGON'S BLOOD TREE
YEMEN

Hundreds of years ago, apothecaries and alchemists would buy hardened lumps of deep red "dragon's blood" to use in their recipes and medicines. It came from the remote island of Socotra, in the Indian Ocean, where the Dragon's Blood tree grows. When cut or damaged, this strange-looking tree leaks a bright red resin, giving it its name. According to old legends, dragons once lived here, and the first Dragon's Blood tree sprang up on the spot where a basilisk (see page 14) fought with an elephant and their blood spilled and mingled on the ground.

ANCIENT DRAGONS

When did dragons first appear? Nobody knows, but we do know that people have been telling each other stories about them for thousands of years. There are dragon legends from ancient Egypt, ancient Greece, and Mesopotamia (the area that is now Iraq), home of the ancient Sumerian civilization.

TIAMAT AND MUSHUSSU

These two dragons appear in many Mesopotamian myths and artworks. In a creation story called the Enuma Elish, Tiamat was an ancient goddess married to the god Apsu. They were the parents of many more gods. But when these gods turned against Apsu and killed him, Tiamat was furious. She took the form of a giant sea dragon and gave birth to a horde of monsters.

TIAMAT

MUSHUSSU

One of these monsters was another fierce dragon, Mushussu, who had a scaly body and tail, four feet with sharp claws, a long neck, and a dragon's head with a forked tongue. The god Marduk fought and defeated Mushussu, who then became his loyal servant and steed.

DRAGON OF THE UNDERWORLD

In the myths of ancient Egypt, which date back to 3000 BCE, Apep is an evil serpent-dragon who lives in the Underworld. Each day, the Sun god Ra sails his boat across the sky, and each night, he disappears below the horizon and must travel through the Underworld. There, Apep lurks, waiting to catch and swallow Ra. Each night, Ra, or one of the other gods, manages to kill Apep—but when they return to the Underworld the next night, he has been reborn.

THE HYDRA OF LERNA

This ancient Greek dragon was a many-headed water monster that dwelled in the sacred lake of Lerna, an entrance to the Underworld. According to myths of the hero Hercules, he tried to kill the Hydra by cutting off her heads, but each time he cut one off, two more grew back. Not to be outdone, Hercules asked his nephew Iolaus to help him. Each time Hercules cut off a head, Iolaus used a fiery torch to burn and seal off the neck, so no new heads could grow—and in this way, the Hydra was finally defeated.

ANCIENT DRAGON ART

Many old rock carvings and cave paintings around the world show animals that resemble dragons—but it's sometimes hard to be sure what they were supposed to be.

This one is from the Valley of Fire in Nevada, USA, where the rock art is up to 4,000 years old.

The Rainbow Serpent is a reptile featured in Aboriginal Australian religious stories. In this rock painting in northern Australia, it looks something like a dragon . . .

This dragon decoration made from clamshells was found in a tomb in Puyang, China, and is thought to be 6,400 years old.

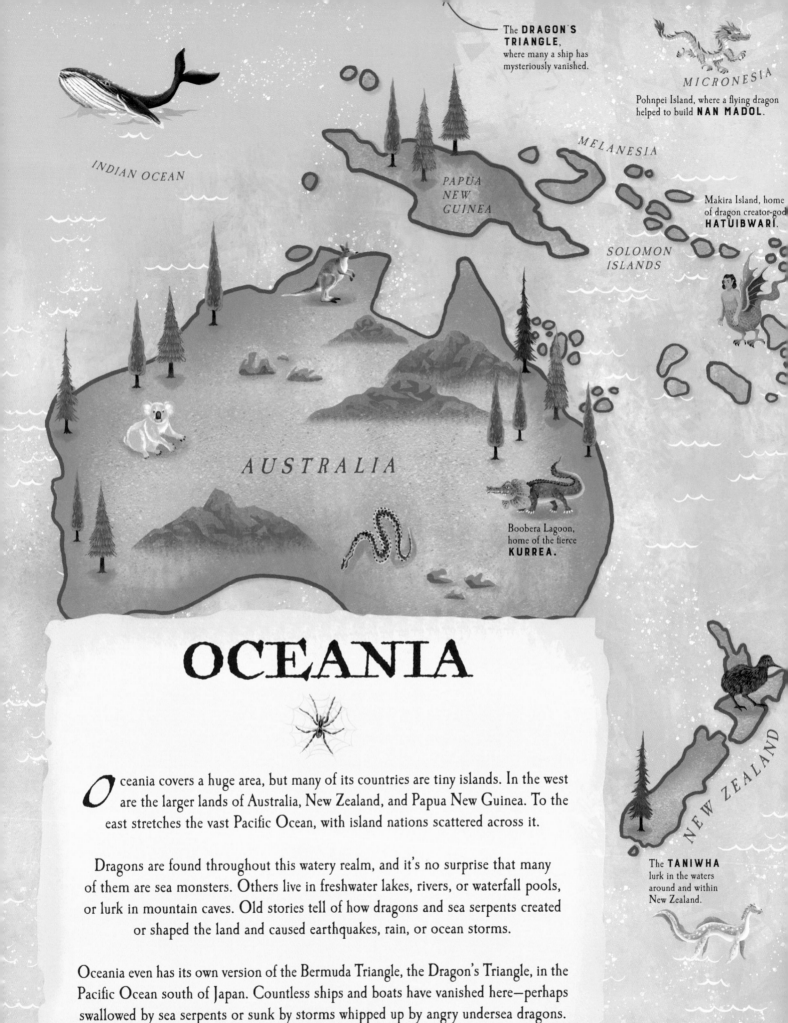

The **DRAGON'S TRIANGLE**, where many a ship has mysteriously vanished.

MICRONESIA

Pohnpei Island, where a flying dragon helped to build **NAN MADOL**.

INDIAN OCEAN

MELANESIA

PAPUA NEW GUINEA

Makira Island, home of dragon creator-god **HATUIBWARI**.

SOLOMON ISLANDS

AUSTRALIA

Boobera Lagoon, home of the fierce **KURREA**.

OCEANIA

Oceania covers a huge area, but many of its countries are tiny islands. In the west are the larger lands of Australia, New Zealand, and Papua New Guinea. To the east stretches the vast Pacific Ocean, with island nations scattered across it.

Dragons are found throughout this watery realm, and it's no surprise that many of them are sea monsters. Others live in freshwater lakes, rivers, or waterfall pools, or lurk in mountain caves. Old stories tell of how dragons and sea serpents created or shaped the land and caused earthquakes, rain, or ocean storms.

Oceania even has its own version of the Bermuda Triangle, the Dragon's Triangle, in the Pacific Ocean south of Japan. Countless ships and boats have vanished here—perhaps swallowed by sea serpents or sunk by storms whipped up by angry undersea dragons.

NEW ZEALAND

The **TANIWHA** lurk in the waters around and within New Zealand.

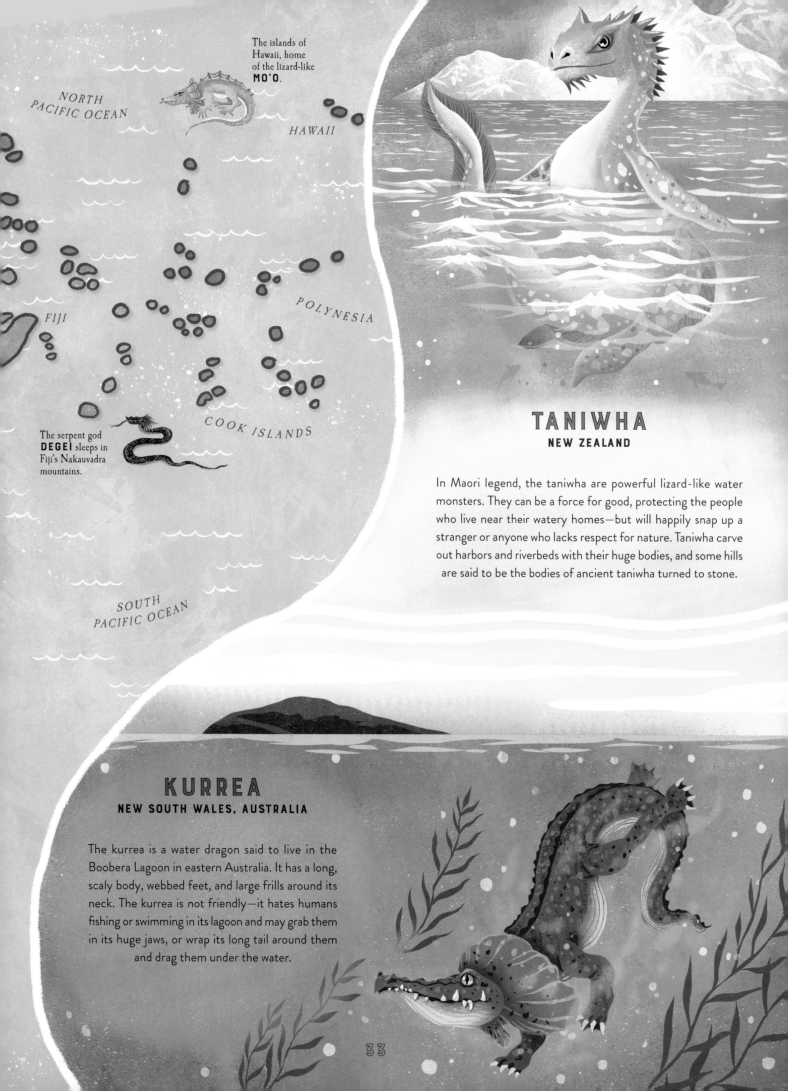

The islands of
Hawaii, home
of the lizard-like
MO'O.

NORTH
PACIFIC OCEAN

HAWAII

FIJI

POLYNESIA

COOK ISLANDS

The serpent god
DEGEI sleeps in
Fiji's Nakauvadra
mountains.

SOUTH
PACIFIC OCEAN

TANIWHA
NEW ZEALAND

In Maori legend, the taniwha are powerful lizard-like water monsters. They can be a force for good, protecting the people who live near their watery homes—but will happily snap up a stranger or anyone who lacks respect for nature. Taniwha carve out harbors and riverbeds with their huge bodies, and some hills are said to be the bodies of ancient taniwha turned to stone.

KURREA
NEW SOUTH WALES, AUSTRALIA

The kurrea is a water dragon said to live in the Boobera Lagoon in eastern Australia. It has a long, scaly body, webbed feet, and large frills around its neck. The kurrea is not friendly—it hates humans fishing or swimming in its lagoon and may grab them in its huge jaws, or wrap its long tail around them and drag them under the water.

DEGEI
FIJI

Long ago, according to Fijian folklore, there were just two beings: Degei, a giant serpent-dragon, and Turukawa, a hawk. When Turukawa laid two eggs, Degei guarded and warmed them until two tiny humans hatched out. Degei formed the islands of Fiji for the humans to live on, grew fruit trees for them, and showed them how to farm and cook with fire. These first two humans gave rise to the Fijian people, and although he is now very old, Degei is still said to watch over them from his nest in the Nakauvadra mountains.

HATUIBWARI
SOLOMON ISLANDS

This mighty dragon god is said to be the creator of the sea, the land, and all the humans, and feeds every living thing that he creates. Also known as Agunua, Hatuibwari has a long reptilian body, with the shoulders, arms, and head of a human. He has four eyes, leathery bat-like wings, and claws instead of fingers. His sacred tree is the coconut palm, and the first coconut picked from any tree should always be left for him.

NAN MADOL
POHNPEI, MICRONESIA

Nan Madol is a mysterious ancient city built on a coral reef in the sea near Pohnpei in Micronesia. No one knows why it was built or how people moved the massive 43 ton (50 tonne) boulders the city walls stand on. However, a local legend has the answer. It tells of how twin wizards named Olisihpa and Olosohpa moved the stones for the city with the help of a flying dragon, who levitated the boulders through the air.

KALAMAINU'U, THE MO'O

SURFING DRAGON GODDESS OF HAWAII

HAWAII

The Mo'o are water dragons said to live in ponds, streams, and deep, dark pools. Many are female and can shapeshift between different forms, appearing as a giant lizard-shaped dragon, a tiny gecko, or a beautiful woman.

A famous story tells of Kalamainu'u, a Mo'o who lived in a river cave on the island of Oahu. One day, she took the shape of a beautiful woman to go surfing on the sea and look for a husband. There, she fell in love with a young chief, Puna-ai-koa'e. Entranced by her beauty, he followed her to her cave, and they were married. Afraid that Puna might find out that she was really a Mo'o, Kalamainu'u kept him prisoner.

But when he begged her to let him go surfing again, she agreed—as long as he spoke to no one.

However, on his way to the sea, Puna met two men, Hinalea and Aikilolo. They told him that his wife was a Mo'o and warned him that one day she would eat him. Puna returned to the cave, and there he saw Kalamainu'u in her true dragon form. In a great rage, she chased Hinalea and Aikilolo, but they turned themselves into wrasse fish, jumped into the sea, and disappeared into a crack in the seabed. So Kalamainu'u made a trap to catch them. Ever since, people have asked her for help when they go fishing for wrasse, and she is said to make sure their traps are always full.

MISTAKEN FOR DRAGONS

For many centuries, people around the world have told each other dragon tales or lived in fear of the dangerous dragons said to dwell in nearby lakes or caves. So, it's no surprise that sometimes people thought they had seen dragons, when they had really spotted something else . . .

TRAVEL TALES

In ancient times, people rarely traveled far, and those who did often came back with fantastic tales or wrote books about their adventures. Some of these stories and books contain fascinating descriptions of dragon-like beasts.

MARCO POLO'S TWO-LEGGED SERPENTS

In the 1200s, Italian adventurer Marco Polo journeyed across Asia. He later wrote about the bizarre dragon-like beasts he saw in Carajan, now known as Yunnan in China. With a long snaky body, two short legs, and huge eyes, they sound very much like dragons. However, some think that Marco Polo actually saw crocodiles but didn't notice their back legs!

Here are seen huge serpents, ten paces in length . . . near the head, they have two short legs with three claws like those of a tiger, with eyes larger than a fourpenny loaf . . . and jaws wide enough to swallow a man.

HERODOTUS AND THE WINGED SERPENTS

In about 450 BCE, ancient Greek writer Herodotus described a strange sight he saw on a trip to Buto in Egypt. There, he was shown skeletons of "winged serpents." One explanation is that Herodotus could have seen the fossilized bones of pterosaurs, flying reptiles from the age of the dinosaurs.

The form of the serpent is like that of the water snake; but he has wings without feathers and as like as possible to the wings of a bat.

DID DRAGONS COME FROM DINOSAURS?

Some people think that dragon legends around the world could have been sparked by fossilized skeletons and footprints left behind by dinosaurs and their extinct relatives. When ancient people discovered them, they might have thought they had come from magical monsters who were still living somewhere in caves or under the sea. Several different types of dragons do seem to match various types of extinct reptiles.

Some have wings, like pterosaurs.

Some have four legs, with birdlike claws, huge heads, and teeth.

Some swim in the sea and resemble long snakes with four small limbs.

Dragons' horns are similar to some dinosaur and pterosaur crests.

LIVING DRAGONS

Some real-life dragons really do roam the wild to this day—or at least, they're *called* dragons!

The Komodo dragon, the world's biggest lizard species, lives on a few islands in Indonesia.

Draco (meaning "dragon") lizards are small lizards from Asia that can glide a short distance on "wings" of stretched skin. They look like colorful baby dragons!

Sea dragons are Australian fish that resemble dragons.

NORTH AMERICA

The continent of North America stretches from the icy frozen tundra in the north to the sweltering tropical islands of the Caribbean in the south, surrounded by the Pacific and Atlantic oceans. This is an ever-changing land of earthquakes and volcanoes, mountains and rivers, great forests, lakes, and sweeping wildernesses—perfect habitats for dragons.

The cultures of these lands reflect their many Indigenous peoples, each with their own stories of magical and fearsome monsters. More recently, migrants and settlers from across the world have come to live here, bringing their own dragon legends with them.

Flying, horned, and feathered serpent-style dragons are common in this continent, though you'll find many others, too, from razor-toothed lake monsters to ravenous dragon-birds. Many of them are deadly, so always keep an eye on the sky and the water, and take care near creepy, gloomy caves.

ALASKA

Beware the cunning **TIZHERUK** near the coast of Alaska.

CANADA

The mist-breathing **AMHULUK** lures its victims here.

USA

MEXICO

PACIFIC OCEAN

GUATEMALA

GREENLAND

HUDSON
BAY

Watch out for
GAASYENDIETHA
flying over Lake Ontario.

Don't get snatched
away by the scary
SNALLYGASTER!

Here, you can find the
mysterious **PIASA**
dragon—or is it a bird?

ATLANTIC OCEAN

CUBA

HAITI

Yucatan, home of
KUKULKAN,
a flying feathered
serpent god.

CARIBBEAN SEA

GAASYENDIETHA
LAKE ONTARIO, CANADA AND USA

The Gaasyendietha, or meteor dragon, is a giant dragon
said to live in Lake Ontario, one of North America's Great
Lakes. According to the local Seneca people, this dragon
came to Earth from space, riding on a meteor or shooting
star. Though it lives in the lake, it can fly and breathe fire,
too. Whenever you see a shooting star in the sky above
Lake Ontario, it's the Gaasyendietha soaring through the
sky on a trail of fiery flames.

TIZHERUK
ALASKA, USA

Stories passed down by the elders of the Inupiat people of Alaska
tell of a terrifying sea monster, the Tizheruk. With its huge head
and snapping jaws, it can gobble up a human in seconds. There
are varying descriptions of the rest of the Tizheruk's body: Some
say it has six legs, some two; some say it's furry like a seal, others
report it has ghostlike, transparent skin. Take care when you
venture out onto a pier or jetty, since the Tizheruk can leap out
of the waves to snatch its unsuspecting victims.

AMHULUK
OREGON, USA

In Kalapooia folklore, the terrifying Amhuluk lives in and around a lake in the mountain forests of the northwestern United States. This creepy-looking creature is covered in fur, with four legs, a spiny back and tail, and two large horns. Wherever it goes, it breathes damp, poisonous mist that spreads disease and sorrow, and the ground beneath its feet softens and turns to slimy, sticky mud. The Amhuluk will capture any animal or human that dares to go near it and drag them into the lake. There, they are transformed into strange unknown creatures and doomed to live with the Amhuluk forever.

SNALLYGASTER
MARYLAND, USA

When people from Germany settled in eastern North America in the 1700s, a scary legend grew up about the terrifying Snallygaster. Its name comes from the German words *schneller geist*, meaning "quick ghost," but it was actually a flying monster, half-dragon and half-bird. It had enormous wings, a beak filled with sharp teeth, and claws of shining metal. It was said to swoop down and snatch farm animals or children from the ground, carrying them away to devour in its cave. The only thing it feared was a seven-pointed star, so people used to paint these on their barns to keep the Snallygaster away.

PIASA
ILLINOIS, USA

On a cliff face overlooking the Mississippi river in Illinois, there's a painting of a monster known as the Piasa. It's a replacement for an older rock painting that has now been destroyed, but was seen and described by explorers in the 1600s. They wrote about a black, green, and red creature with a scaly body, a human-looking face with horns and a beard, and a long tail with a fishy fin at the end. Though it's sometimes called the "Piasa bird," the mysterious monster looks more like a dragon. It's thought to be part of the folklore of the Cahokia people, who lived in the area a thousand years ago, but no one knows for sure what it was or whether it was a friend or a deadly foe.

KUKULKAN

MAYA HORNED SERPENT GOD, BORN TO A HUMAN FAMILY

MEXICO

The Maya people have lived in the Yucatan area of Mexico for over 4,000 years. In their ancient beliefs, the most important god was Kukulkan, a winged serpent with a dragon-like head. Sometimes, he shapeshifted and appeared as a human Maya warrior or a giant snake with a human head or face.

To this day, Maya people tell stories about how Kukulkan was born. Long, long ago, a human family had a baby, but he was born as a snake. His big sister took him to a cave, where she fed and cared for him. As the snake-boy grew bigger and bigger, he developed feathers and horns, and his sister could see that he was no ordinary snake, but a feathered serpent god.

Eventually, her brother became so huge that she could no longer find enough food for him. He spread his wings, flew out of the cave, and away across the sea. As he went, a violent earthquake shook the world. The serpent had become Kukulkan, the powerful god of earthquakes, rain, wind, and storms, as well as farming, war, and all life, including life on Earth and in the Underworld. Since that day, every summer, he makes the Earth shake again as a message to his sister that he is still alive.

DRAGON SIGHTINGS

W hat would it be like to spot a real-life dragon circling in the sky or lurking in a cave or murky lagoon? It may seem strange, but many people, from long ago to modern times have sworn that they really have seen a genuine dragon. Let's investigate . . .

ALEXANDER THE GREAT'S DRAGON

This ancient Greek king and army leader was said to have encountered a dragon during his travels in India. According to a description in an ancient Roman history book, the giant serpentlike monster hissed loudly and stuck its head out of a cave—and its head alone was around 30 yards long! Locals worshiped the beast and begged Alexander not to attack it, so he didn't. What Alexander saw is a mystery, but no known land creature could be that big!

THE DRAGON OF BOLOGNA

In 1572, there were reports of a small, hissing two-legged dragon roaming the countryside near the Italian city of Bologna. According to a naturalist named Ulisse Aldrovandi, a local herdsman found the dragon and killed it. Aldrovandi himself then claimed to have collected the dragon's dried body and displayed it in his nature museum in Bologna. Since it was so small, he said that it must be a baby dragon!

Experts say that the dragon seen in the museum could have been a hoax made from a snake, a fish, and the front legs of a toad stitched together. But could there still have been a real dragon sighting?

THE ARIZONA WINGED MONSTER

In 1890, a local newspaper in Tombstone, Arizona, reported on an incredible monster encounter: Two cowboys had chased and killed a monstrous beast they found in the desert, which seemed to be exhausted from flying. It resembled an alligator with an extra-long tail, two legs toward the front of its body, and two huge wings. When measured, it was said to be 92 feet (28 metres) long. However, no one seems to have collected, studied, or preserved the monster's body.

A WELSH MINI-DRAGON

Dragon sightings have even continued into the twenty-first century. In 2001, biologists explored a quarry in Wales to look for a strange animal described by locals. They were amazed to see a yard-long dragon-like beast, flying around in a circle. It was said to be shimmering green, with a head like a seahorse. It has not been reported since.

THE DRAGONS OF MOUNT PILATUS

Mount Pilatus in Switzerland is associated with many dragon legends and at least three reported dragon sightings.

Even to this day, it's said that on Mount Pilatus, you can sometimes hear the flapping of dragons' wings or see their shadows on the rocks.

In 1421, a farmer reported seeing a dragon flying toward the mountain, swooping so close to him that he fainted from its intense heat and terrible smell. When he woke up, he found a stone covered in dried blood nearby, which was later said to have magical healing powers.

In 1499, the morning after a violent storm, a drenched dragon is said to have climbed out of the Reuss river near the Spreuer Bridge in Lucerne, near Mount Pilatus. Some said it must have been swept down a mountain stream by the high winds and rain.

And in 1619, local politician Christophorus Schere wrote, "I saw a very bright dragon with flapping wings, flying from a cave in a great rock in Mount Pilatus . . . Its head was that of a serpent with teeth, and sparks were coming out of it."

SOUTH AMERICA

South America is a vast triangle-shaped continent, thousands of miles wide in the tropical north and narrowing to a curved dragon-like tail as it stretches toward Antarctica in the south. This is a land of extremes, from the towering ice-capped Andes mountains to the vast, hot and humid Amazon rain forest. Here is the world's biggest river, the Amazon; the biggest waterfall, Iguazú Falls; and the highest active volcano, Ojos del Salado.

Though Ojos del Salado hasn't erupted for more than a thousand years, South America has many volcanoes that have erupted much more recently, such as Cotopaxi and Villarrica, and their lava-filled craters make a perfect home for fire-loving dragons. Dragons are also said to dwell in jungles and forests, rivers and caves, or in a mysterious underground realm.

As well as breathtaking wild landscapes, South America has an amazing array of astonishing wildlife, such as the anaconda, a giant water snake; the condor, a giant bird of prey; and the common basilisk, a lizard that can run on water and resembles a tiny dragon. Perhaps these creatures share their natural homes with dragons—or at least helped to inspire the many dragon myths and legends found across this great continent.

COLOMBIA

The Amazon rain forest, is home to countless wild creatures . . . and dragons.

AMAZON RAINFOREST

Take care not to step on the slow-moving SACHAMAMA.

BRAZIL

PERU

Peru and Bolivia are home of the mighty dragon AMARU.

BOLIVIA

ANDES MOUNTAINS

CHILE

ARGENTINA

Ojos del Salado, the world's highest active volcano.

The IHUAIVULU dwells in volcanic craters.

PACIFIC OCEAN

Beware of the scary PEUCHEN.

Chat with an ARAGANAQLTA'A in Argentina.

SURINAME

MAZON RIVER

The gleaming-eyed
BOITATÁ guards
Brazil's forests.

IGUAZÚ FALLS

ATLANTIC OCEAN

IHUAIVULU
CHILE AND ARGENTINA

In the folklore of the Mapuche people, the Ihuaivulu is an enormous fire dragon, with a snakelike body and seven heads that constantly spit out flames. It dwells in the craters of active volcanoes, where it can easily start a deadly eruption whenever it chooses. It's also said to guard the entrance to the Mapuche underworld, a land of serpents. The Ihuaivulu is covered in red shining scales, and some say it makes these itself by melting copper in the searing heat of its volcanic home.

PEUCHEN
CHILE AND ARGENTINA

Another of the many legendary creatures of the Mapuche people is the Peuchen. It most commonly appears as a serpent with colorful, feathery wings, and it makes an eerie whistling sound as it flies. The Peuchen preys on sheep and goats, and sometimes humans, paralyzing its prey with its gleaming, golden eyes. Then it swoops down and sinks its fangs into its helpless victim to suck all their blood—and their heart—from their body.

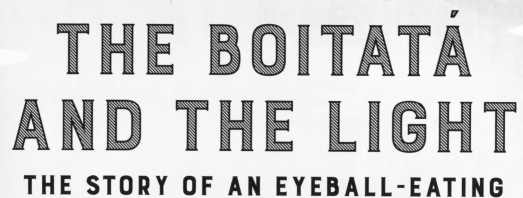

THE BOITATÁ AND THE LIGHT

THE STORY OF AN EYEBALL-EATING SERPENT-DRAGON

BRAZIL

The Boitatá is a dragon-like magical creature of the forest in the legends of the Tupi and Guarani peoples. Its name means "fire snake," and it's said to be a giant horned serpent that glows with flames, especially from its eyes, which blind anyone who sees them.

The Boitatá was not always like this, however. Long, long ago, it was an anaconda, a huge water snake. One day, the sky turned dark, and heavy rains began. The rain kept falling until the whole world was flooded, and thousands of wild animals were drowned. The anaconda emerged from its home and roamed around, eating the eyeballs of all the drowned animals it could find, which shone in the darkness.

The more glowing eyeballs it devoured, the more brightly it began to glow itself, until it was a monstrous, light-filled serpent. But although the eyeballs made it shine with light, they did not provide enough food to keep it alive, and at last, the snake died. Its body burst open, and all the light inside it was released back into the world and became the Sun in the sky. The forest was no longer dark, the trees flourished, and the jungle became a home for the animals once again.

But the serpent was not gone. It became a glowing forest spirit, the mighty Boitatá. To this day, it prowls the jungle, guarding the wildlife and setting fire to anyone who tries to harm the trees—and, of course, eating their eyeballs.

AMARU
PERU AND BOLIVIA

The Amaru is an important and all-powerful dragon in Inca and Tiahuanaco folklore from the mountainous west of South America. It has a scaly serpentlike body, a fish's tail, the wings of a condor, and two heads; one a bird, the other a jaguar. It lives deep underwater or underground, and its body of many parts represents its power to combine different worlds: the water and the underworld, the land and the sky. It provides water for humans, but it can also bring lightning storms and floods, earthquakes and fires, and change of all kinds.

ARAĠANAQLTA'A
ARGENTINA

This beast of Toba folklore usually appears as a giant serpent, crawling on long fringe-like parts that run along the sides of its body. On its head is a red crest, which gives it magical powers. It has two hooks on its tail, used for holding prey. It can appear in other forms, too: As a four-legged dragon, a flightless rhea bird, or even a human—but whatever shape it takes, it will still have a crest on its head. The job of the Araġanaqlta'a is to protect nature, and it will attack anyone who damages the wild forests, rivers, or living creatures. However, if you behave respectfully, then it will be your friend, talk to you, and teach you the power of healing.

SACHAMAMA
PERU

In the rain forests of Peru lurks one of the biggest of South America's serpent-dragons, Sachamama, or Mother of the Forest. She's a giant reptile with a huge lizard-like head and stone-gray scales. When she opens her mouth, it looks like a cave. Sachamama lies still in the jungle for hundreds of years, until trees grow on her back, and it's easy to mistake her for the ground. But when she does move, she shakes the whole jungle, carving massive muddy channels as she slithers along. Beware: Although Sachamama can be friendly, she is also likely to snap up and swallow any human who annoys her.

DRAGON GUIDE

As every dragon-spotter knows, while some dragons are harmless or even friendly, many are not. If you should ever meet a dragon, this useful guide tells you what to do to make sure you return alive and well.

RESPECT NATURE

- Many dragons guard wild places, especially forests and lakes. These nature guardians will only attack you if you behave badly, so respect the natural world at all times.

- Don't burn the Boitatá's forest, invade the kurrea's lagoon, or sail your boat too close to the Mokele-Mbembe.

- Step carefully wherever you go, just in case a dragon lurks nearby.

PROTECT YOURSELF

If you know what a dragon fears most or how to outwit it, you'll improve your chances. Remember:

- A seven-pointed star will scare away the vicious Snallygaster.

- A magic orange tree can guard against a dragon's fiery or poisonous breath.

- The deadly basilisk is terrified of weasels, the only kind of creature that can kill it—so always take a weasel with you when dealing with this dangerous dragon.

DRAGON-FIGHTING

Fighting a dragon should always be avoided if possible. But if you have no other option, these tips may help:

- Your sword or spear will probably be no match for a dragon's iron-hard scales. Instead, aim for its softer scale-free belly or armpit.

- Trick larger dragons into eating a sulfur-stuffed sheep or some burning peat.

- Don't do a deal with a dragon! They can be sneaky, as Dobrynya Nikitich learned when he fought the evil Zmey.